Mom, Pop, and Tot

TEACHING PALINDROMES

BY MARY LINDEEN

The Child's World®
childsworld.com

Published by The Child's World®
1980 Lookout Drive • Mankato, MN 56003-1705
800-599-READ • www.childsworld.com

ACKNOWLEDGMENTS
The Child's World®: Mary Swensen, Publishing Director
Red Line Editorial: Editorial direction and production
The Design Lab: Design

Photographs ©: Shutterstock Images, cover, 1, 2, 4, 6–7, 9, 10–11, 12, 15; iStockphoto/Thinkstock, 12–13

ISBN 9781503808393
LCCN 2015958431

Printed in the United States of America
Mankato, MN
June, 2016
PAO2304

ABOUT THE AUTHOR

Mary Lindeen is a writer, editor, former elementary school teacher, and parent. She has written more than 100 books for children. She specializes in early literacy instruction and creating books for young readers.

A palindrome is a word that reads the same forward or backward. Look for **palindromes** in this book. You will find them in **bold** type.

This is the home of the **Otto** family. They live on the top **level** of this tall building.

This is **Eve Otto**.
She is the **mom**.

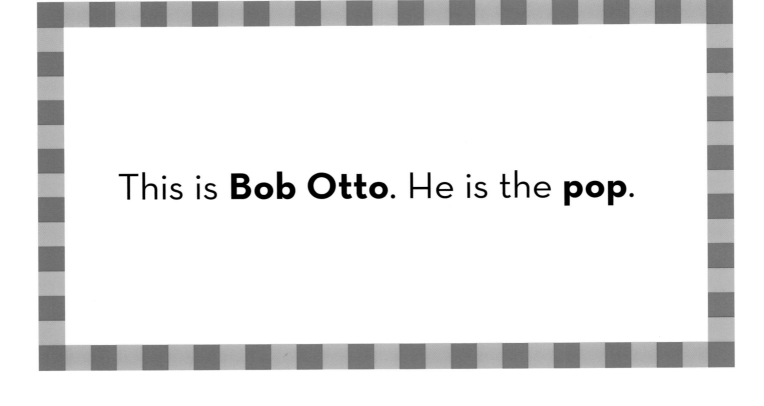

This is **Bob Otto**. He is the **pop**.

The little one is **Anna Otto**. She is their **tot**. **Anna** is asleep, so she does not make a **peep**.

Anna likes to play with her **racecar**. Sometimes she plays her horn in bed when she should be sleeping. **Toot**! **Toot**!

Today at **noon**, **Anna** made a big mess in her bedroom. **Mom** and **Pop** need to keep an **eye** on their **tot**!

Did you find these palindromes?

Anna	Otto
Bob	peep
Eve	pop
eye	racecar
level	toot
mom	tot
noon	

To Learn More

IN THE LIBRARY

Agee, Jon. *Palindromania!* New York: Square Fish, 2009.

Collins-Matza, Carol. *The Palindrome Kids.* Mustang, OK: Tate, 2015.

Shulman, Mark. *Mom and Dad Are Palindromes.* San Francisco: Chronicle, 2014.

Terban, Marvin. *Too Hot to Hoot: Funny Palindrome Riddles.* Boston: HMH Books for Young Readers, 2008.

ON THE WEB

Visit our Web site for links about palindromes: **childsworld.com/links**

Note to Parents, Teachers, and Librarians: We routinely verify our Web links to make sure they are safe and active sites. So encourage your readers to check them out!